Stories of

PASSING

STRANGERS

*sharing a moment
can forever change a life*

featuring stories by

Garry Hojan

Melody Morgan   Crystal Thieringer

Catherine Mulholland   Terri Gillespie

and Kay Haggart Mills

Edited by Angela Hunt

Hunt Haven
Press

Published by Hunt Haven Press
Seminole, FL

Cover design by Angela Hunt
Photo © olly-Fotolia.com

ISBN-13: 978-0692317778
ISBN-10: 0692317775

EDITOR'S NOTE

The idea evolved slowly, but once it bloomed, it made perfect sense. Why not sponsor a short story contest to echo the theme of my latest novel, *Passing Strangers*? After all, in 1987 I published my first book because I entered a contest . . . and after all was said and done, a nine-year-old boy selected my story as his favorite.

So I announced the contest on my blog, and entries trickled in over the summer of 2014. Because some of the entrants were friends, I asked my book club members to judge the entries, and they judged manuscripts marked only with numbers, not names.

And now I'm happy to present the top six stories. Garry Hojan, a newcomer, took the top honor, and I'm honored to be his first publisher. I hope you will enjoy all the stories from these fine writers.

Angela Hunt

CONTENTS

ACKNOWLEDGEMENTS

Thank you to our contest judges:

Cathy Stock
Gina Presson
Barbara Drews
Laurie Norris
Deshay Milas

1 FROM A STAIRWELL TO A FUTURE

Garry Hojan

Judge's comment: "The author paints a graphic picture of the desperation of this runaway child from the first words of the story."

Find a warm place or die. That's how I felt and all I could think about. My aching fingers were not making it any easier to stay focused; they had been frostbitten two years earlier when I was twelve. That seemed a lifetime ago and so far from where my mind was right then, all I wanted to do was get warm. My whole body convulsed from the cold.

So much hurt. Why wasn't someone coming to take care of me? Did I have such little value that my own mother would choose a violent alcoholic, who wasn't even my real father, over me, her youngest son? After all, if it weren't for him I wouldn't have ended up like this. Tears stuck my eyelashes together. I couldn't see. My mind raced as I tried to figure out how to save myself on my first night being on the street.

I had wandered through the shopping malls earlier in the day to stay warm. Now they were closed. I walked for hours, trying to stay warm. Something made me keep moving. I knew stopping in this weather might mean the end of me.

It was hours after midnight when the thought of a warm

apartment stairwell come into my mind. I don't know what made me think of it, other than maybe memories of warm stairwells in the apartment buildings my mother, brother and I lived in when I was younger.

Pain, cold, and snow made walking difficult, but the thought of warmth made me pick up my pace and head toward some apartments along the road. I went from apartment building to apartment building, hoping that one would have an unlocked door. None did. When I got to the last apartment in the row, I tried the lobby entry door. It was locked.

It was too late to try and pretend to be a person needing to get into the apartment building, so if I buzzed someone's apartment I would alert suspicion. I couldn't stay in the lobby; I would get taken away and possibly get taken into custody. I had spent time in a foster home and did not want to go back to that.

Seems silly writing those thoughts now: Die or go back to a warm foster home.

I went back out into the biting cold, that wonderful eastern wet cold that cuts through whatever you are wearing and finds your bones.

I went to the back of the apartment building, I nervously looked over my shoulder, took my social security card out of my pocket, and began to try and jimmy the lock. It opened right away. It crossed my mind that this was easier than I thought it would be, but more important, I felt the rush of pungent apartment air—*warm* air. I slipped inside and headed to the stairwell, then went to the very top of the staircase where the roof access was, one floor above the last floor of apartments.

I had an alarm clock in my pocket. Whatever possessed me to keep an alarm clock with me? I sat on the concrete floor, completely exhausted and scared, but at least I was warm. I set the alarm clock for a few hours from that moment, and drifted in and out of sleep, interrupted by every sound and my own heightened guard. When the alarm went off, I crept down the staircase, running back up a level every time I thought I heard someone. I would wait, listen, and move until I finally made it downstairs, then I slipped out of the building into the crisp pre-dawn air.

The malls weren't open yet, but The Donut Hole, affectionately known as "The Hole," was. This was where students hung out, some innocently playing a game of pinball and grabbing a sandwich, many skipping classes, smoking, or dealing dope. For me, the place meant warmth and people—even if some of them made me nervous.

I knew some of the kids. We had graduated junior high together just last summer, so having familiar faces around comforted me.

This became my routine: hang out at The Hole during the day and go back to the apartment stairwell at night. Stella, a small Filipino-looking woman, owned The Hole. Every once in a while she would let me clean off the pinball machines and would feed me a roast beef sandwich. Sometimes she would talk to me, ask me where I live, don't I go to school? I don't remember how I answered, but I was thankful someone was taking an interest in me. I can almost taste those sandwiches—they were like the sweetest manna to me.

There were others like me, kids on the street. I didn't hang out with them. I knew them, but something kept me from forming any bonds with them. I spoke with one of the guys I knew and he told me they had broken into a vacant townhouse so I was welcome to crash there. I didn't want to stay with them, but thought maybe the house would have a working shower. After being on the street for a time, you get, um, to smelling *ripe*, and I was definitely beyond that point.

Their routine was to go in after dark and leave before daylight, not turning on any lights in the house. I opened the unlocked door and gagged from the stench, but went in anyway. I went into the bathroom and found the source of that smell. I tried to flush the toilet, but there was no water.

Having no father and always being curious, I read a lot and learned about things, including how systems work. I knew there had to be a water shut-off valve somewhere in the house, so I turned that on, then the water heater, and then went back upstairs and flushed the toilet. I left the house and went back to my stairwell that night, knowing that water heater would not heat up for quite some time. I didn't want to risk being in a house where someone might see or catch me.

The next night I went back to the townhouse. It smelled a bit better. I locked myself into the bathroom and took a hot shower. A simple hot shower, but the sheer joy of that simple thing is hard to describe. That shower washed away the shame I felt from being dirty.

I sat and air-dried until I could dress. Other kids were in the house by then. I warned them about staying too long and left for my stairwell, again not wanting to risk being caught in the house. I heard the next day that they had been found out. Some were taken away by the police, while others got away.

There was this girl who would come to The Hole from time to time. I had noticed her but didn't know her, and there's no way I would actually talk to her. She was strikingly beautiful, just gorgeous, with blonde curls and a cute face. I was painfully shy and filled with self-loathing. I had developed catlike reflexes to keep from getting hurt, plus I was always on point and got involved with people just enough to have some human association, but no connection. I had become a master at protecting myself, so I just stood there when she walked up to me and said "Hi, I'm Liz— Elizabeth—but you can call me Liz."

Liz asked me some more questions. I guess she knew I was on the street and had noticed me, then she asked if I wanted to come home with her.

I stood in a dumbfounded state for a long time, probably looking as dopey as I ever had, while I asked myself why such a beautiful angel would ask me to go home with her and meet her parents.

Something pushed me to say okay. Honestly, it was probably hormones, but food would have done it, too. Her tenderness moved something in me.

Liz's home was a real home, with real home sounds, sights, and smells. I could smell good European cooking. Her dad was a sturdy man and her mom had a soft, caring look to her. I was cautious, but so wanted to believe this to be real. I didn't trust at all, so when they set up a cot for me in the basement I was hesitant. When I accepted and went to bed, I didn't sleep. My mind was alert and wary, but thankful nonetheless.

The next day the family had a large meal and invited me to take part. Liz told me they had a surprise for me. I didn't like surprises and started thinking about how I could get out of there. Here it was, the surprise I was wary of. They were going to turn me over to the authorities, and "do me some good." No way! I wasn't going back down that road. I would rather be on the street. I decided that when the time is right, I was out of there.

I could barely enjoy the great food because I was so wary. Liz's dad could easily overpower me. Could I make it out the door before he could tackle me? When he said, "Elizabeth told us you have a brother out west in Edmonton?," I nodded.

"We've bought you a plane ticket to fly to be with him. Would you accept that from us? We would like to help you."

Why would they do that? I had already gone through the University of Mistrust in my life, and couldn't believe the news at first. Then they showed me the ticket.

I don't remember if I cried then, I only know that as I write this, I find the memory moving. They fed me, washed my clothes, and gave so much more. They gave me money and took me to the airport. How much love that family had, how much giving in their hearts. They changed my life through their grace and kindness, possibly even saved it, and I never will forget what they did for me.

That was thirty-six years ago. About five years ago I found Liz, that passing stranger, through social media. I let her know how grateful and thankful I was for what her family did. I told her that I considered her my guardian angel from God, and she saved my life. She told me that I elevated her too high, and that she brought me home to get the "bull's-eye" of her parents' attention off her back and onto mine. We laughed over that one.

I let Liz know how I had come to the Lord, then met and married God's gift for me, my wife Julie-Ann. I asked if there was anything, anything at all, that I could do for her family. She said it was enough to know I was doing fine.

I am amazed at how God works His plan. I knew He had watched over me, but I didn't know about the other side to this story.

Earlier this year Liz told me that her dad had passed away. She said they had talked about me one last time and she told him about me contacting her. He was happy to hear that I was doing well.

Liz said her dad understood my situation because he experienced his own loneliness when he immigrated to Canada. He escaped from a war alone while the rest of his family was captured. "I think he was very happy I dragged you home instead of another cat or dog," she said. "But more than anything, he was happy he could help you with what you needed at the time. I have never said this to anyone, but now I am posting it . . . after you got on the plane and we went home, he had tears in his eyes—something a proud man never has. He really cared. He knew you were a good kid. And like I said, he was happy to know now you are a successful man in all aspects of life."

Somehow, God used my season of trials to help someone else.

> Look at the birds of the air, for they neither sow nor reap nor gather into barns; yet your heavenly Father feeds them. Are you not of more value than they? Which of you by worrying can add one cubit to his stature? So why do you worry about clothing? Consider

the lilies of the field, how they grow: they neither toil nor spin; and yet I say to you that even Solomon in all his glory was not arrayed like one of these.

Now if God so clothes the grass of the field, which today is, and tomorrow is thrown into the oven, will He not much more clothe you, O you of little faith? Therefore do not worry, saying, 'What shall we eat?' or 'What shall we drink?' or 'What shall we wear?' For after all these things the Gentiles seek.

For your heavenly Father knows that you need all these things. But seek first the kingdom of God and His righteousness, and all these things shall be added to you (Mathew 6: 26-33).

And sometimes, the Lord can do this through a passing stranger.

2 A STRANGER'S ULTIMATE GIFT

Melody Morgan

Judge's comment: "This story was touching. The beginning grabbed your attention immediately, with fear that someone has passed."

Rrriiinnnggg!!! The sound sent my heart racing. Large red numbers on my alarm clock forebodingly flashed 4:30 a.m. I leaped out of bed and lunged across the room to the spot from which the noise came. My whole body trembled from fear of who might be on the other end of the telephone.

"It can't be time!" My wide eyes searched the dark for my husband. "They said it would be months. It's only been five days!" I could taste bile rising from my churning stomach. I frantically grabbed the receiver and held it to my ear. I heard beeps and alarms from monitors in the background that confirmed my fears.

"I need to speak to a parent of John Mark Walker, please." The voice on the other end seemed hurried and matter-of-fact.

"This is Melody, John Mark's mom," I squeaked out. I was barely able to hear my voice over the freight train roaring through my chest.

"This is Arkansas Children's Hospital and we have found a heart to match your son. You need to get here

8

immediately."

I sank to my knees, my body crumpling along with my courage. I cried out to God, "I'm not ready! We haven't had time to prepare."

My husband wrapped his arms around the lump I had become on the floor. "This is what we've been praying for. God's timing is perfect," Jerry said. His words were a soothing balm to my soul. "Let's pray and thank God for this wonderful gift."

As Jerry prayed, I began thinking of the donor's mother. She must be devastated at the loss of her child. As much fear and uncertainty that I was feeling, how much more of a burden must she be carrying? I could not imagine the heart-breaking pain she had to be enduring. I knew only God could give her the peace and grace she needed to cope with such a loss. I claimed Psalm 34:18 for this precious mother. *The Lord is near to the brokenhearted and saves the crushed in spirit.*

"Lord, be with this mother in her time of desperation. Thank you for bringing her into our lives. Help her to cope with the life-changing decisions that she is making," I earnestly prayed.

Nine year old John Mark was anything but fearful when we woke him with the news. He immediately called family and friends and invited them to his heart party in Little Rock. "Guess what?" he asked everyone on his call list. "I'm getting my new heart today! Meet me in Little Rock. Now I will be able to run and play without stopping to breathe!"

John Mark was born with a severe congenital heart defect in which the left side of his heart did not form correctly. He had multiple surgeries in the first few years of his life to help restore heart function. His cardiologist warned us that a time would come when John Mark's heart would not be able to sustain his growing body. That time had come. His heart function had declined and John Mark had been placed on the national transplant list on August 16, 2002. Five days later he received the gift of life: a beautiful, perfectly beating heart.

John Mark has had no rejection symptoms since his

transplant. He leads a happy and healthy life. I'm forever grateful to our passing stranger for choosing refuge for others in the midst of her storm.

A day never passes that I don't think about this mom. I wrote the following poem for her while John Mark was in the hospital following his transplant. The nurses assured me they would send it to her.

Gracious Gifts

Early morning of August 21st in the blackness of still night,

We were awakened by the call that brought many emotions, initially one of fright.

"A heart has been found for your son John Mark." I trembled, as from fear I grew weak.

I knew that from this moment on for strength, my Lord must I seek.

I'm not ready, I pleaded, and do I have to do this? Please Lord, take this burden from me.

"My child," He softly and tenderly spoke, "My grace is sufficient for thee."

And then my thoughts were instantly turned to the place where this heart would come.

I thought of the mother and the love she had; where did her strength come from?

Were we both praying to God up above, "Lord, help me see Your will?"

Touch me with Your loving hand and Your peace within me fill.

Throughout that day I was often reminded of the gracious gifts that were given.

How God must have felt when His son

died so that we might have life in Heaven.

That mother also gave a tremendous gift so that another's child might live.

She gave the very gift of life, what greater gift could one give?

I'm thankful to my God, my King. He sacrificed all for me.

And thankful to the mother who gave, so more life my child may see.

3 A NEAR-MISS BLESSING

Crystal Thieringer

Judge's comment: "I especially liked the use of metaphor and anthropomorphism. The dialogue rings true as well."

The fact of the matter is this: that car should never have been close to the road. And I shouldn't have been behind the wheel.

But then again, 1983 was defined by bad decisions. One resulted in a sternly-worded reprimand from the Dean himself, and another led me to the Finance Department, where I was schooled in the realities of needing more than talent and sarcasm to get through college. They expected to be paid for the privilege of my attendance. My bank account held $27.13, an amount acceptable only if I could hip-check the decimal point several digits to the right.

Since I'd learned the path of least resistance from my parents, I decided not to tell them I was coming home. I knew they wouldn't send me back—they couldn't afford my school bill, either. I imagined how they might explain the mess to their friends.

"Remember we told you our daughter went to college? She dropped out two months before graduation. We've never been so proud."

Lacking both the emotional fortitude for that conversation and the funds for more glamorous options, I made the decision to drive nine hours across the Canadian prairies. Alone. In winter.

Dad had bought the car from his oldest friend. He never touched it, never saw it. She was delivered to me in January, and I ignored the rust and rattles because of her precious keys. I loved what she represented enough to name her. Little Red Corrie would provide needed transportation. More importantly, she would help me hide from all the blissful college kids I never seemed to fit in with.

It mattered not that her past owner thought she was a roller derby blocker. And didn't everyone use their parking brake to stop at a light? There was no reason to use the back door that wouldn't open, and I didn't mind sticking my arm out the window before I turned left. Heat was a relative term, and that window frosted up too much anyway. I could always add extra layers—something I was quite used to doing. Having grown up in Saskatchewan, I was well acquainted with what its winters could toss my way.

Corrie and I rumbled along for a few weeks until she adopted a California Girl attitude about the cold, and got cranky about starting. Still, when I faced my unexpected road-trip, I challenged her to show what she was made of.

She did.

I stuffed her nooks and crannies with every precious possession. My friend taped eyes and a smile to the guitar case, and it became my passenger. A quick hug and a "Ready, Guitar?" later, I turned Corrie's key.

Nothing happened.

Another colleague who knew a thing or two about cars encouraged the hood to stay open while he worked on the engine. Corrie grumbled like a teenager on a school morning. He said, "I don't know, Crystal, but if I were you, I wouldn't stop this car."

Maybe that's what I heard. Maybe what he said was, "Only a suicidal idiot would attempt to drive this caricature of a vehicle across the parking lot."

The day was drizzly for February, making the highway shiny and the windows grimy. Corrie's windshield wipers kept metronome time until a few kilometers out of the city, when she flung the passenger side wiper into the ditch.

"Apparently we don't need that," I said to Guitar. "Good thing it wasn't on my side, or I'd have to stop for sure." Even so, I pulled over often to rub sloppy snow over the blurry glass. My credit card—finally good for something—scraped the window clean again.

Two hours later, I gurgled fuel into the tank. "Please start, please start, please?" I prayed.

To my relief she did, though not without a coughing spasm. We navigated through Saskatoon but at the edge of the city, Corrie had a debilitating asthma attack. I pulled into a parking lot and she reclined across two spots.

"She thinks she's a Lamborghini," I said to Guitar. No amount of my coaxing would break Corrie's stubborn silence.

I called an older woman I knew in town, and she in turn arranged for the services of her Vehicle EMT. Once Corrie was revived, he said, "Crystal, try not to turn her off until you get where you're going."

That sounded familiar.

At least six hour's drive-time remained. Six hours to determine how—and how much—I was going to tell my parents. About the financial mess? Everything. About the man I let use me because I believed he loved me, even after I found out he'd finessed the same lines on every girl in school? Yeah, I'd probably leave that bit out.

Since the radio didn't work, I drove with few distractions.

Which is probably what saved my life.

With a horrendous bang the left rear tire burst, careening Corrie and me across on-coming traffic and into the ditch on the other side of the two-lane highway. Shaking, shivering, shuddering, I couldn't pry my fingers off the wheel.

A percussive rap at the driver's side window should have startled me but instead, the sound tiptoed into my brain. I turned my head to see the concerned face of a stranger. His neck was protected by a dark grey scarf as he leaned into the car, away from the wind. I lowered my window an inch or so.

"You okay there, Miss?" he said.

I lied, assuring him I was. "Sorry!" I said. "I don't know what happened. I almost got hit by that car."

"That car," he told me, "was mine. You cut right in front of me. Did you blow a tire or something?"

I nodded. "I guess," I said with a tremulous voice. "I'm so sorry."

He shrugged. "We're all okay, right? Let me help you fix it. Got a spare?"

Good question. It hadn't occurred to me I might need one. He grimaced when he saw the discombobulation in the trunk—an oversized IBM Selectric typewriter, garbage bags of clothes and bedding, my flute, and a tumble of theory and theology textbooks inhaled the space.

"Well, it should be under here," he said. He hefted a bag of clothes and opened the passenger door. Guitar startled him. "It's got a face," he said, looking at me as though wondering if I knew.

"Yeah," I said. "That's Guitar."

For the next five minutes we stacked the remnants of my life on the shoulder of the wet road. He retrieved the tire from some hidden recess under the floor of the trunk— another secret Corrie had kept from me. It took all his weight on the wrench to free the rusted lug nuts. "Hmm," he said. "You really should get new rims."

"Yeah, I have to get home first," I said. "I left school because I couldn't afford it anymore and I was living on hopes and dreams and there was this guy and—" I kicked the mud flap, wondering why I'd blurted that out.

He put a hand up to stop me. "Don't do that while it's up on the jack, okay? Not safe." Breath fog wafted around him. I hugged myself as I paced behind him, wishing for some place to sit.

"This should take you as far as you need to go," he said,

"but don't ride on it anymore than that. It's not designed for it."

Corrie grumbled when I asked her to start. I grumbled back. Then the stranger helped me get out of the ditch, calling instructions through the open window while he pushed the car, his feet slipping in the slushy trails left behind as we climbed.

Once the blown tire was put in the spare's hideaway, we reloaded the trunk. Where my packing style had been strewn and scattered, his was geometric precision. I removed my sodden mitten and reached for his gloved hand. "I don't know how to thank you," I said. "I really don't."

"Just get home safely. Here." He pressed a fifty dollar bill into my hand. "Take this, okay?"

"I couldn't possibly—"

"Yes, you can. Accept the gift. That's how to thank me."

Embarrassed and tearful, I waved as his tail-lights winked at mine. It was another five minutes before I realized I hadn't even asked his name.

For the next three hours, I rehearsed my explanations with Guitar. "I couldn't make enough money teaching flute," I said. "Not enough students. And my own lessons cost too much." I'd leave out the part about jerk-man. "It's going to be okay."

Except, it wasn't.

Corrie gave an epileptic swerve, yanking hard to the right. I wrestled her to the shoulder while she burbled and bobbled. The vibrations caused by the flattened tire rattled the car so much that Guitar fell towards me, clunking my shoulder. I shoved it against the window when the car stopped.

"Why?" I banged my hands on the steering wheel, causing Corrie to give a wheezing toot in reply. I didn't have another tire. I had no way to contact anyone. I wasn't sure I'd get her going again if I turned off the engine. "Why, why, why?"

I sobbed and shivered. If I didn't thrust my frozen feet back in the snow to walk to the closest town, someone would find my body cuddled up to a bemused guitar case. What a eulogy that would be.

I left the car, unlocked by Corrie's choice, and made my way along the road. My boot-prints were a magnet for the falling snow, and I sniffled as I walked.

Sunday afternoons shut down small towns. The garage, the corner store, and the library were all closed. I saw a post office attached to a house, and desperately hoped the postmaster would be home. I banged on the door, and a woman's pinched voice called out.

"Yes?" she said through the frosted glass. Apparently she thought I was a serial killer, thief, or degenerate. She refused to let me past the porch.

"Please," I begged. "I just need to call my dad. I can give you the number and you can call collect, and I'll stay out here, but otherwise I can't get home. Please."

After a moment of silence, she said. "Number?"

I recited it to her through the glass door. A few moments later, the door opened wide enough to pass the telephone handset through. I looked at the tip of her slipper as I contorted against the short length of the cord.

"Dad," I said.

"Hi." He seemed distracted and I realized I'd called right in the middle of a hockey game. "How's things?"

"Not so good. I'm stranded. Blew out the tire. I need a new one."

"Well, put the spare on," he said.

"Can't. I'm already riding it."

"Grab the bus then, and I'll fix the car later."

I winced. Stupid hockey game. "Dad, please?" I tried again. "Everything I own is inside and that car doesn't lock."

"Everythin' you own? What about school?

I took a step back and looked at the handset as though it had betrayed me. "I'll explain when I see you." My voice wavered. "Dad, this lady wants her phone back. Can't you bring a tire and come get me?"

The only answer was the muted sound of cheering. Dad apparently watched the replay.

"Dad?"

"Okay," he sighed. "Be right there."

A wrinkled hand stuck through the door, and I returned the phone to the slipper's owner. On the slog back to Corrie, I calculated that Dad would need just under two hours to arrive. I'd have to pull out dry socks from my designer garbage bag, and maybe another sweater, but I'd be okay. I was annoyed that Dad had needed so much convincing, but he's a man who dislikes inconvenience only a little less than confrontation, and I was asking him to accept both. On game day.

I pulled out my ugly yellow Walkman and popped in a Keith Green tape. I figured the battery would last most of the waiting time. The words "Run to the End of the Highway" filled my earphones and I laughed. "I would if I could," I said to Guitar.

I closed my eyes and sang along, waggling my head and beating a funky counter-rhythm on the steering wheel. An uneasy feeling of being watched made me look out to the right. I practically ejected from my seat. Big eyes stared back at me, and then a hand motioned for me to roll down the window. I reached across and turned the handle a quarter-turn.

"Hi," he said. "I'm Sean. My mother sent me to stay with you."

"Your mother?" I snorted. "Wow, that's original."

"No, really. You just used her phone."

I was not in the mood for company, even—or perhaps especially—a guy with a dimple kissing the right side of his mouth. Especially one whose mother thought I was a serial killer.

"There's really no room to sit," I said, gesturing at Guitar.

"I was thinking my truck?"

"No," I said, "I'm good."

He grinned. "Okay. I tried. Take care."

"You too. Thanks."

As he drove away, I debated my decision. A warm place to

sit and wait was appealing. Small talk was not. And I didn't know him.

"I'm not even sure I know myself anymore," I said to Guitar.

I anxiously scanned the horizon for Dad's green Ford pick-up. One hour turned into two. I imagined Dad in his garage salvaging a tire. As two hours turned into three, I knew he had possibly gotten distracted in that job. Shivering, I shielded my eyes from the sun peeking in the top of my windshield.

Another truck appeared before Dad's did though. Sean had returned. "Cold enough?" he said. "C'mon. I brought cocoa."

This time I changed vehicles. I appreciated the warmth of the hot chocolate. The silence was awkward and after a few hesitations, Sean said, "You think your dad's coming?"

"Of course he is," I said. "He'd never leave me here. How dare you accuse him of that!" How could I explain that Dad is a putterer, often late because scuzzy garage things distract him? That is, if he wasn't caught up in overtime.

Sean raised his hands. "Slow down, that's not what I meant. But if you thought he'd been in an accident and you wanted me to go look for him—"

"An accident?" I hadn't thought of that, and fought against the bile in my throat. "No," I said, squinting at the horizon. "He probably just got held up in the traffic . . ." My voice trailed off. I was no longer sure.

It was dusk before Dad arrived. I introduced him to Sean.

"Hey, got a joke to tell you," Dad said, because that's how he copes with uncomfortable. Sean laughed politely while Dad yanked a tire from the truck bed.

"Sir," said Sean, "that's not going to fit." He pointed to the number of hub-holes. My car needed four. The tire Dad borrowed from Mom's car had five.

Dad looked at me somewhat helplessly. "Could just leave it," he said, pointing to Corrie.

"All my stuff—"

"Hey," said Sean. "We own the gas station. I can swap the rims for you for . . . let's say, sixty dollars."

Dad looked at me again. "No, we—"

"Would you take fifty dollars?" I said to Sean. I fumbled for the bill the stranger had given me earlier. "Here. It's all I have." Dad frowned at me. Apparently, I'd pre-empted another "deal".

"Follow me," Sean said.

It was another hour before I was able to turn Corrie's key again. Naturally, she muttered and stuttered before giving in. "We have to stop for gas," I said, taking note of the station Dad said to use. I pulled out ahead of him, comforted by the knowledge that he was tailing me.

"You're missin' a left turn signal, and you're wanderin' all over the place," Dad said as we filled up. "Why are you drivin' like that?"

"Because this evil piece of junk is demon-possessed." My words chased each other. "Why didn't you check it out before you stuck me with her? Why didn't you see if she at least had brakes so I wouldn't have practically killed someone. Or tires! I hear they're useful. Why'd you make me sit in the field with some guy I don't even know?"

It wasn't my finest moment. Neither was the one that matched it when Corrie and I finally jerked to a stop in our driveway. I slammed the driver's door, and I'm sure she winced. "I'll take my stuff out tomorrow," I said to Dad. "Do what you want. I'm never touching her again."

Within a week the car was gone.

I know now that Corrie wasn't Dad's fault. He trusted someone he shouldn't have. The argument that followed permanently damaged a decades-old friendship.

There were several arguments those days, among them a negotiated return to finish the semester—though that didn't happen for three more years. In the meantime, my relationship with dimply Sean and his odd mother ended with a thank-you note sent in care of the post office.

Of course, I never saw the stranger I almost collided with

again. I've often wished I knew his name so I could properly thank him.

But perhaps I have. In moments when I'm prodded to help another, I never doubt the rightness of it if my brain also flashes a memory of a little red car on a prairie two-lane. Maybe the best way to thank this kind of stranger is to become one.

4 STRONG LOVE

Catherine Mulholland

My head leaned uncomfortably on a pillow I had stuffed against our old van window. Occasionally Old Blue hit a pothole and my head pitched to and fro, leaving comfort under mild duress.

Outside a blur of neutrals, greens and oranges swam beneath blue sky. I trained my sight on each moving object and tried to follow each one from the front of the van to the back, but found no success. The repeated motion did, however, succeed in shipwrecking my stomach and frying my vision.

Two of my brothers goaded one another incessantly from the back seat. They had their own special language of burble, mutter and garble; only they understood it. My brothers were peculiar that way. They just "got" one another: had an understanding that enunciation was only for formal occasions.

I zoned in and out of the boys conversation—just enough to make me cognizant of guy talk. Atari games, dirt bike riding, basketball and the like were always on the list of welcome discussion topics. I rolled my eyes and let out a sigh. I was disinterested with the world and more importantly, with life. It had only been mere days . . .

My parents had separated suddenly. Mum had loaded the family van and trailer overnight while dad had driven to another town with his brother to gamble on racing dogs. Dad had been distracted; mum had been determined. With one travel bag, mattress, and chest of drawers per person, my mum, my bothers and I fled town.

On the trip to our new hometown we stopped once for refreshments, as my youngest brother was severely disabled and needed constant care. No one ventured a cheery disposition, as the situation was gloomy no matter which way we looked at it. New schools. New house. New town. New friends. In fact, in order to accept the enormity of change upon us, we had each (in our own way) recognized that fleeing had been necessary for our own safety. We had become anonymous citizens. No traceable phone number. No daily routines. No advertised address. No credit cards. We were off dad's grid.

Then we were headed to Melbourne. It was the middle of summer and the Aussie sun was relentless in its gaze. As usual, the air conditioning in Old Blue had decided not to work. Our legs swam on the vinyl seats and our faces said *hot and bothered.*

A scorching wind whipped the top of our hair through half-cracked windows. The edges of my frustration began to wear thin. Having already driven through several small, distanced towns, I was ready for a break. One that consisted of chilled water and food.

Mum flicked at Old Blue's indicator and we tick-tocked our way on to a heavily shaded park trail. I wound my window down and leaned out for a better look.

The park was sheltered by large gum trees above and blanketed by velvet below. A creek bubbled and gurgled to one side and its banks smelled earthy and nutty. As we pulled to a stop, a cooled breeze calmed our skin and brought a welcome reprieve.

"Ok kids, go and play while I get lunch ready!" Mum exited the car.

I slid from the front seat of the van to the second row, next to my little brother. It was too hot to play. Daniel, my youngest brother, sat stiff and still. His unbalanced gaze was fixed upon the park that lay beyond Old Blue's windows.

A brief smile danced across Daniel's face, followed by a squeal of delight. Daniel did that sometimes. On occasion we had considered the possibility that Daniel had seen Angels. His whole countenance would suddenly light up upon seeing something nearby that we could not see.

"Come on Daniel," I said, unbuckling his special car seat. "Let's get you out of here because it is lunchtime."

I pulled Daniel out of his seat, complete with facial cloth, and carried him over to the closest shaded picnic table. Daniel was heavy, and at thirteen, I wasn't that strong.

Matthew and Jim followed us over, offloaded a partial loaf of bread, some spreads and some water. They then took off running, shoving and goading one another on their way to the play-set.

My mum wandered over with Daniel's diaper bag, her mind still replaying our departure from several days ago. She was obviously making an attempt to gain composure and put on a brave face, but there was no denying that our new reality was completely daunting. Mum was now a single parent with no income, no home furnishings and no idea as to how we would make it through the week, let alone to Melbourne. Daniel had to see a specialist, though, so there was no way we could not proceed.

Mum pulled several slices of bread from the plastic wrap, deep in thought.

"Hello! I'm—"

Mum and I both startled and turned toward where the voice had come from. A man stood close by and extended his hand toward us in greeting.

Mum seemed startled at the intrusion, so I introduced myself – and her. "I'm Catherine and this is my mum."

"Hi, I'm Terri," Mum said.

The man bowed lower to extend a special greeting to

Daniel. "And who is this?"

"This is Daniel." My mum wasn't too sure what was transpiring, yet I could tell from her countenance that she did not feel uneasy in any way. There was something different about this man.

"My wife and children and I are eating lunch over there." The stranger turned and pointed to a table behind us filled with family, food, and light-hearted conversation. "We were wondering if you would like to join us? We've plenty of food to go 'round."

"Um . . ."

I could tell that mum was about to say no, but the stranger interrupted her. "Terri, we would love to fellowship with you and your family!"

"Ok." My mum sounded hesitant, but curious at the same time. "We would love to, but we have nothing to bring to the table."

"No worries—come on over! We have plenty of food."

And with that, we spent the better part of the next hour fellowshipping with perhaps one of the most loving and inclusive families we had ever met. When our appetites were satiated and our host family was ready to leave, we said our goodbyes and thanked the family for inviting us.

Mum packed everything into the back of the van once again, as I carried Daniel back to his car seat and strapped him in.

"Jimmy! Matthew! It's time to go now!" My mum walked around the side of the car to slide into the driver's seat. Just as she closed the door, the strange man's wife walked up to mum's window to speak with her. I am still not sure what was said, but I could tell that it deeply touched my mum as she wiped away several tears from her eyes.

While I watched the exchange take place by driver's seat, the stranger appeared beside me at Daniel's window. He tapped on it lightly and stuck his head through. With a smile on his face, he whispered, "Can I please have your hand?"

I gave the stranger my hand. Again, he whispered, "It was

lovely meeting you all today. God wants you all to know that He is going to look after you." The man slipped something into my hand and closed my fingers around it. "You give this to your mum when you are a little further down the road. Don't tell her you have it until you've left town, ok?"

I nodded, a little dazed and confused. "Thanks," I said. "It was nice to meet you, too."

"You all take care, ok? You tell your mom that God knows your needs and He will supply them."

I climbed out of the middle row and back into my seat in the front passenger side. With my seat belt firmly around my waist and my hand full of something curious, I could not rest my head on the pillow. Something amazing had just taken place.

As we drove further down the road, I shifted my gaze downward and unclenched my fist. There, folded into halves, was money!

I cannot recall how much money was in my hand, but I do remember that when Mum saw it, she was overjoyed. Relief flooded her face and stress fell away. "Our trip to Melbourne and Daniel's treatment is paid for, Catherine!"

I wish I could remember the name of the stranger and his family we met that day. But though I cannot, I can remember their strong love in the midst of our season of grief.

5 PASSING STRANGERS UNDER A TRAY OF BREAD

Terri Gillespie

Judge's comment: "Beautiful! This really caught my heart!"

"Watch the back of the person in front of you!" Our Israeli guide, Areleh shouted above the clamor of street vendors. "Watch it or you'll get lost!" As coordinator of this Israel tour, I had a vested interest in watching not only those in front of me, but *everyone's* back.

Keeping ninety-one awe-struck tourists together—and on schedule—was like herding toddlers in the best of circumstances. My challenge became all the more daunting as we circumvented the narrow streets of Jerusalem's Arab Quarter, over an hour behind schedule.

It was Ramadan, the Muslim high holy days. Our delay meant we were now caught in the surge of men emerging from the mosques and women making last-minute purchases for the family's breakfast. The constricted corridor intensified the aromas of baked bread, fish, and unwashed bodies.

What was a group of Jewish and non-Jewish believers in Jesus doing in "inhospitable" territory? Poor timing, according to Areleh—too many bathroom stops, chats with

Israelis, and souvenir acquisitions. As a retired IDF colonel, his concern to impel us through this area had less to do with schedule and more about our safety.

My husband, Bob, and I brought up the rear of our herd like sheepdogs, barking directions to "move on", "stay together", "no stopping" and "hurry up, for goodness sake." All the while the locals eyed us suspiciously.

I pasted what I hoped was a carefree smile on my face and prayed out loud, "You parted the Red Sea, Lord, how about this sea of humanity?" But the street only grew more congested.

Honestly, I was scared. It was one thing to hear gunshots fired by exuberant Muslims during Ramadan while safe in a hotel, but vastly different being in their neighborhood as uninvited visitors.

Up ahead I spotted a young man of about twelve or thirteen carrying a four-by-three-foot tray of baked goods on his head. He maneuvered his way—against the current—toward us. How he moved at all was a wonder.

A silly idea bubbled up inside me. As he approached, instead of backing away and letting him pass, I ducked under the right side of the tray. A millisecond later, crouched next to the young man, the tray a few inches from my head, I glanced to my left and came face to face with a Muslim woman—also crouched, also head inches from the tray of bread.

We made eye contact. Her cocoa brown eyes twinkled. We both broke out laughing.

My brain snapped a mental photo. She wore a tightly wrapped gray *hijab* around her round, olive-skinned face. Numerous lines and wrinkles nestled on her forehead, and around her eyes and mouth. Her arms clutched a bundle tight against her breast. Worn and crooked teeth graced her smile. She was beautiful.

Not a word passed between us, only laughter. Yet, we connected.

As quickly as it happened, it ended. Time moved us on—

back to our responsibilities. I soon lost sight of her in the moving mass of people.

As Bob and I exited the Arab Quarter through the Damascus gate—our herd intact—my heart felt light, my smile sincere, and the fear had disappeared. When I attempted to share the "meeting" with others, I received tepid responses—you know, the kind adults give a child who thinks every pebble is a treasure. I couldn't blame them. I didn't understand what had transpired myself. I only knew my heart warmed with something sweet and this Muslim woman had a part in that.

I am a second-generation Christian Zionist. My husband's family has a Jewish heritage. For me, scripture is clear: Israel belongs to the Jewish people. While I don't believe a Palestinian state is scriptural, I believe the Palestinian people—as do most Israelis—have the right to live and prosper in Israel peacefully with their Jewish "cousins."

My prayer for the peace of Jerusalem and Israel as a whole is a regular petition. Since the Intifada began in 2000, the second Lebanon War, and the Gaza battles, I have prayed for all victims of terrorism and war, as well as those who fight for our country.

Had I wished ill for the Palestinian or Muslim people? Absolutely not.

Did I hope they would come to salvation? Absolutely.

So what was different?

The tour continued with more adventures. God brought other Arabs into my path as never before in our previous trips to Israel—remarkable encounters like a Muslim restaurant owner who went from ranting about the impossibility of peace to fixing me a fruit smoothie as we discussed God's peace. Or the Christian Palestinian archeologist we regularly visited, who had recently brought a terrorist to the Lord.

While in Jordan we met a storeowner in Petra who wanted to marry our daughter (she was flattered, but respectfully declined), and too many young beggars who should have been in school—one young man so eloquent, I could see him as class president or valedictorian. After awhile the encounters felt divinely orchestrated.

Once we returned home to Pennsylvania, our much too busy lives resumed. The memories were set aside for more pressing responsibilities. Even the mental photo of that special moment with the Muslim woman whom I came to think of as "my friend" began to fade.

As director of operations for a Messianic Jewish ministry, I returned to my life in the Jewish community. Managing the domestic operations of our humanitarian efforts to Israel's poor—Jews, Arabs, Christians, and Muslims—consumed my days. More than ever I felt good about our efforts to help Arabs and Muslims. Like my friend.

But God didn't want this event to be about my warm fuzzies.

A few months later, I attended a technical conference in Texas. Organized by a Christian company, the conference ended with a lovely banquet and keynote speaker, Stephen Saint. I had never heard of this gentleman. According to the bio on each table, the speaker's father was Nate Saint, known as the "Jungle Pilot," one of five missionaries killed in 1956 by the Waodani Indians, considered one of the most violent tribes in the world.

The bio resonated with me before the lanky man wearing jeans and cowboy boots walked to the podium. With a soft voice he humbly shared his testimony.

After the brutal death of his father and friends, Stephen's aunt and other missionaries were miraculously invited by the Waodanis to live with them. Within a few years the gospel message of love and forgiveness transformed the tribe. Shortly after, at the age of ten, Saint met the men who killed his father and friends.

God's transforming message of love and forgiveness impacted Saint as well as the tribe, for he not only grew up among these men, he came to love them and regard them as family.

One tribesman, Menkye—whom Stephen believed to be the man who actually killed his father—"adopted" him. Today, Stephen's children call this tribesman "Grandfather." Menkye played a pivotal role in Saint's revelation of his Heavenly Father's heart.

Saint finished his testimony. We stood and applauded—a few wiped away tears. Afterward a group went forward to talk with him and buy his book, I went back to my hotel room and wept. Understandably, I was moved by his story, but it seemed there was more I was to take away from his message.

Flying back to Philadelphia, my head spun with technical and spiritual matters. Monday morning I shared Stephen's message with one of my staff. Kimberly, an outspoken Messianic Jewish woman, responded, "Well, that would be like me calling one of the terrorists who chopped off my dad's head 'Father!' That's deep!"

That *was* deep. It was also the connection to all these encounters God had orchestrated.

Instead of seeking God's insights, I had romanticized the encounter with the Muslim woman—an occupational hazard for a writer. I must admit to imagining her sharing our story with everyone in the Arab Quarter. That she thought of me fondly and with wonder, as I did her. Thinking that perhaps she even missed me, of all things.

But, what if her son strapped on a bomb and blew up a bus full of children? Would I still fondly remember that experience? What if she killed my daughter? Would I still call her "my friend"?

Could I truly forgive and adopt her into my heart as a sister given the same circumstances as the martyred missionaries?

The Saint family actively demonstrated that it *could* be done. Not only that it could be done, they risked everything to do it.

God opened His heart to me and compared it to mine. How mine lacked.

He reminded me that before I believed in Jesus I was His

little girl. Didn't that apply to my friend? Wasn't she someone He longed to lovingly wrap in Jesus' Robe of Righteousness to be His forever? How He would grieve if that transformation didn't take place?

His open heart showed me that my motives for praying for the Palestinian and Muslim peoples' salvation was more for the safety and peace of the Jewish people and Israel than true compassion for their immortal souls. He wanted me to see and experience that. To fully understand their passionate inclusion into my heart in no way usurped the Jewish people's place, for He had enlarged my heart—there was plenty of room.

Stephen Saint said God revealed His Heavenly Father's heart in the jungles of South America. I believe that's what my Heavenly Father did to me, under a tray of bread.

He gave me a sweet, beautiful face to my prayers for the salvation of the Arab and Muslim peoples—and as I watch the horrific reports of bombings, tunnels, beheadings, shootings, and pervasive hatred of the Jewish people I'm grateful to have that reminder.

A reminder to hope and pray, with an enlarged heart, that these dear ones will come to know true *shalom*—true peace— with the Prince of Peace. To continue to hope and pray that one-day—if it hasn't already happened—my friend will be my sister.

6 MY GREEK ANGEL

Kay Haggart Mills

Rena was an angel. . . she was sent to me as a direct answer to prayer. Never before have I had a prayer answered so immediately, so completely and so beautifully.

As my husband Bill and I prepared for our trip from western Pennsylvania to Baltimore's Johns Hopkins Hospital, I was suffering from a classic case of mixed emotions. I was grateful that our local doctor had enough knowledge of my husband's problem to refer him to a Johns Hopkins specialist. Yet at the same time I was nervous and apprehensive about surgery in a strange city and strange hospital 250 miles from home.

My anxiety level was high. The thought of having to be the strong one for my husband was frightening. I knew that throughout this whole ordeal I would outwardly have to be strong, supportive, calm and reassuring for him. The actual pain and following post-operative discomfort would be his, but I would need to be there for him in every way. I didn't feel strong or calm.

I had sent up my prayers of concern and protection on my husband's behalf and then almost as an afterthought, I asked, "Lord, could you please send someone for me?" I needed someone who would be there for me, to compensate for my weakness. The surgeon, nurses and other hospital staff would be taking care of Bill. I was completely on my own.

We drove to Baltimore that dreary Tuesday in January 1998, checked into a nearby motel for the night, and then reported to the hospital at six a.m. on Wednesday morning. In a tiny crowded waiting room, many patients and family members waited for the patients to be called to the pre-op rooms.

My husband and an older man were called at the same time. As we gathered up suitcases and tote bags, his tiny dark-haired wife and I looked at each other and agreed that we might as well go get some breakfast. Since her husband had been a Johns Hopkins patient before, she guided me through the maze of hallways to the cafeteria.

We knew it would be quite a while until our husbands were out of surgery, so we talked as we picked up coffee, bagels and cream cheese and cups of fresh fruit from the breakfast line. In a bustling cafeteria, in our booth the conversation continued until we went back upstairs to the family waiting room.

Rena's husband's health problems were more serious than Bill's and this was his second surgery in a short period of time. While Bill's surgery was somewhat routine, we had been informed of possible complications and dire possibilities. To me, anything involving anesthesia is threatening. In the waiting room I knitted, and Rena and I tried to read, but then ended up talking some more.

Finally, our respective surgeons came and reassured us that the surgeries had been successful. Rena and I parted at that point and went to two different parts of the hospital to wait for our husbands to be moved into their rooms. Fortunately, for out of town patients Johns Hopkins allowed spouses to stay overnight in the patient's room. She and I both were grateful for this provision. We were glad that we would not have to deal with the huge hospital, a parking garage and Baltimore traffic.

When I looked for Rena in the cafeteria at suppertime, I

was disappointed to find that our schedules didn't mesh. Fortunately, a gray haired older woman who was there for her sister's surgery joined me as my dinner companion. Again, I wasn't alone.

The next morning after seeing that my husband had had his breakfast, I returned to the cafeteria hoping to find Rena. She was looking for me and greeted me with a smile. Again, we hit the cafeteria line and sat down to resume our conversation of the day before. We weren't able to talk as long this time, because my husband was to be discharged later that morning. Her husband would need to stay a little longer.

I was much calmer that second morning and took a second look at Rena. As we talked I realized that with her long dark hair, her classic black dress, her ornate silver jewelry and heavily accented English, she wasn't just another suburban housewife from Maryland. While I am a life-long Presbyterian with British, German and Dutch roots, her heritage was Greek and her life was intertwined with the Greek Orthodox Church. She and I were contrasts in every way.

However, as we talked I continued to be amazed. She and I were as different as could be but the common threads of wife and mother linked us. We seemed to be about the same age while she was the mother of five and I the mother of three. Our children were about the same ages and we had both daughters and sons. During the time we spent together we talked about anything and everything. We covered hospitals and our husbands' health, or course, but we also found much common ground as we discussed our families, life in general, careers, motherhood, and faith.

Looking back on the time we spent together, I am thankful that God brought this lovely woman to me exactly when I needed her presence in my life. She and her husband had come from Greece to the Washington D.C. area more than thirty-five years earlier. Their odyssey to America brought them to fill music and education positions. That journey of the 1960's provided me with an angel for my anxious heart during those days in Baltimore.

When Rena and I said goodbye that Thursday morning, we exchanged names, addresses, phone numbers and hugs much as two teenagers would at the end of a week of summer camp.

In the course of our conversation, Rena mentioned that her family speaks only Greek at home and Greek is the language used in the school where she teaches. However, there was no language barrier between the two of us. God not only brought us together, he made sure that we could understand each other perfectly. Two strangers in a huge city hospital became strength and comfort for each other.

An interesting post script to this story was the fact that even though Bill's health required two more surgeries and two more trips to Johns Hopkins, I received no other visits from an angel. Rena's presence was an answer to my prayer and visible evidence of divine intervention when I needed it most.

On the return trips to Johns Hopkins I was a veteran. I knew where to go, what to expect and remembered the maze of hallways to the cafeteria. Surgery is never easy—for those who endure and those who wait. But for that first visit, Rena was sent for me. God was with me and so was Rena.

However, on our third and final trip to Baltimore, a new dimension was added to my Johns Hopkins experience when I met a mom who was there with her son. With his shaved head and huge scar, her son Sam was recuperating from surgery for a brain tumor.

His mom had slipped out of his room briefly to sit in the nearby visitors' lounge where I was taking a break and knitting. As conversation followed, I realized that my son Brian was about the same age as her Sam—both were in their mid-twenties. So on a Mothers' Day weekend in 1999, she and I, two strangers, sat hand in hand in the lounge with smiles and tears and talked about fears, joy, faith, hope and the blessings of sons.

We who have been blessed by angels understand.

7 JUST PASSING THROUGH

Angela Hunt

I woke early this past Monday because I had an appointment at 7:40 a.m.

I don't usually schedule appointments that early, but this one was for a follow-up mammogram. The annual x-ray I'd had a week before was "inconclusive," so my doctor sent in an order for a more thorough procedure.

I dressed in the dark and drove to the breast cancer center. I wasn't nervous—I've written novels about breast cancer patients, so I knew what to expect—but I couldn't help realizing that I might soon discover that I had breast cancer. Two of my maternal aunts have had it, so the gene undoubtedly runs in our family . . .

After checking in and being fitted with the requisite wrist ID band, I went to the waiting area. The place was busy despite the early hour, and as I looked around I realized that every woman—and the two men—in that place had stories of their own. I overheard one patient remark that she was coming in for a re-check: if her x-ray proved clear today, she'd be officially cancer-free. I found myself hoping—praying—that she'd have the result she wanted.

The woman across from me wore elastic supports on both knees. She sat quietly, her shoulders down, her hair gleaming in the overhead light. Her haircut was cute, short, and swung easily around her cheeks. But she wasn't smiling. What had brought her to this place, and what procedure was she facing? These aren't the sort of questions you ask a stranger in a medical office, but I wanted to do something for her. After all, we were both tagged and waiting in the same place, facing the same fears . . .

A technician came out and called a name, and the woman struggled to stand up. As she passed in front of me, I lifted my gaze and caught her eye: "You have the *cutest* haircut."

Her fingers rose to touch the hair at the nape of her neck. "You think so? I cut it myself."

I gave her a smile of undisguised admiration. "You do a great job. It really is adorable."

She smiled back, and was still smiling when she followed the technician through a pair of double doors.

I smiled, too.

PASSING STRANGERS

The novel by Angela Hunt

A train roars over the rails, carrying passengers on a trip that will change their lives. Among the many people aboard the 97 Silver Meteor are Andie Crystal, a lonely young woman hiding from her youth as a reality TV star; Matthew Scofield, a widower trying to escape his responsibilities to his two young children; and Janette Turlington, a middle–aged mother running from a situation that has destroyed the peace in her home and marriage. These three form a makeshift family on an Amtrak tour through the Southern seaboard, a journey that just might heal their wounded hearts and restore them to the people to whom they matter most . . .

Available wherever fine books are sold.

ISBN-10: 0692230203
ISBN-13: 978-0692230206

Made in the USA
Charleston, SC
24 October 2014